Encore! Encore!

An Organ Tribute to Fred Bock

Edited by Mark Thallander
Foreword by Kimo Smith

ACKNOWLEDGMENTS: We are grateful to Barbara Heimburger for her copy editing and proofing; to Sonja Maine for coordinating all the loose ends; to David Hempstead for layout and completion; and to Dick Bolks, the world's most wonderful engraver and meticulous musician, a fellow organist and long-time friend of Fred's, for not only engraving, but editing, typesetting, and as Fred always said, "telling everyone how *he* thinks it should be done."

FOREWORD

Fred Bock was a good friend whose generosity was unbounded. It is impossible, however, to speak of him without remembering his wit and offbeat sense of humor. He once presented me with a copy of his composition, "Grand Recessional," written twenty years earlier, which he had rescued from a music store's bargain bin. On it, Fred had written: "To Kimo, who got this for free, not $1.25, which is quite reasonable." He was also interested in my financial success, convinced that this would occur quickly and easily if I would only open an all-night organ shoe store. Fred was an enormous support to me as a performer. Whenever we did choral workshops together, he applauded me as "the best nine-fingered organist I know."

Fred would probably be disappointed to hear that there is still no Loma Linda All-Night Organ Shoe Store offering shoes in liturgical colors—also his suggestion. "Grand Recessional," however, more than paid for itself after one performance. Occassionally, I meet those who seem a bit disappointed to learn that I actually have ten fingers.

It is also impossible to speak of Fred without fond remembrances of our fourteen-year friendship and partnership. Fred's active support of my efforts as a church musician, performer, composer, and family man was a constant encouragement. I could always count on him to call not only to tell me the latest joke, but also to help whenever illness or crisis threatened my family.

In this memorial collection, we honor and thank Fred for being our highly respected colleague and much-loved friend. These hymns of celebration, hope, and faith reflect the way that he lived his life. God is truly faithful, and as the words of Fred's favorite hymn state, He gives us "strength for today and bright hope for tomorrow." One day, God will reunite us with our beloved friend. At that reunion I hope to give Fred a pair of brand new organ shoes—in liturgical white, of course.

With joyous hope and gratitude,

KIMO SMITH

A NOTE FROM THE EDITOR

When the Editorial Board of the Fred Bock Music Company invited me to serve as editor for this collection, I was honored and deeply moved. Working with such gifted people has been a true delight and a once-in-a lifetime experience.

Since it was through Fred Bock that the invitation came for my first organ book, this was a unique way to show my appreciation for that original opportunity. Through the conversations and correspondence related to that first publication, I learned of Fred's humor. His letters were filled with funny statements as he shared the gift of joy—even while at work! Fred often jokingly asked if the Leslie speakers had been added to the pipe organ at The Crystal Cathedral, how many there were, where they were placed, and if the pews could be removed. He thought it would be a marvelous experience to skate in the Cathedral, accompanied by appropriate music from the mammoth pipe organ! He also suggested that people could watch from the balconies.

Fred Bock was a minister of music, a conductor, a worship leader, an organist, a pianist, a producer, a composer, an arranger, a recording artist, and a master communicator. For Fred, however, **church** music was more than music—it was ministry! God gifted Fred with special talents: he was a prophet, bringing God's word through sacred music; he was an evangelist, using intergenerational music to reach the unchurched; he was a teacher, using music to impart God's word; and he was a pastor, a disciple of Christ who lovingly cared for others.

The last telephone call I received from Fred, one week prior to his death, was in his role as a pastor. He took time from his busy schedule to call and to tell me that in leaving my current position, he felt I was following the Lord's direction. After I returned from my vacation, we were to have lunch. Fred was willing, once again, to mentor and encourage me. I will never forget his telephone call, which I believe the Holy Spirit prompted. How thankful I am that Fred listened to that "still, small voice."

Fred Bock was an example to all of us in the music ministry, calling for worship to maintain a balance in musical styles as well as insisting on theological depth. Fred and his companies have provided us with some of the world's finest anthems of praise, hundreds of settings of traditional hymns and gospel songs, and the latest in contemporary expression of faith.

May Fred's brilliant gifts continue to foster meaningful music in this new millennium. And may these new arrangements, which we lovingly present in his memory, assist you in leading your congregation as you worship Almighty God.

With a grateful heart,

MARK THALLANDER

Dedicated to the memory of Fred Bock,
whose faithfulness to his God, his family, his friends,
and his art was an inspiration to thousands

GREAT IS THY FAITHFULNESS

WILLIAM M. RUNYAN
Arranged by FREDERICK SWANN

Fred Bock was a great encourager who used his many talents and his humor to bring out the best in people. He was equally at home conducting a choir, meeting with business associates, or talking one-to-one. I know, because I was often the recipient of his magic touch. Fred was never too busy to offer helpful suggestions, and he was grateful for the smallest returned favor. How artfully he combined kindness with his faith. By now I'm sure that he has collected all the publishing houses in heaven under his umbrella and has the angels rehearsing some new opus. Aren't we blessed that Fred left so much behind for us to celebrate!

Frederick Swann

Solo or Ch.	Chamade (or other loud Reed 8')
Sw. and Gt.	Full, coupled
Pedal	Full without 32', coupled to Sw. and Gt.

Marcato (♩ = 66)

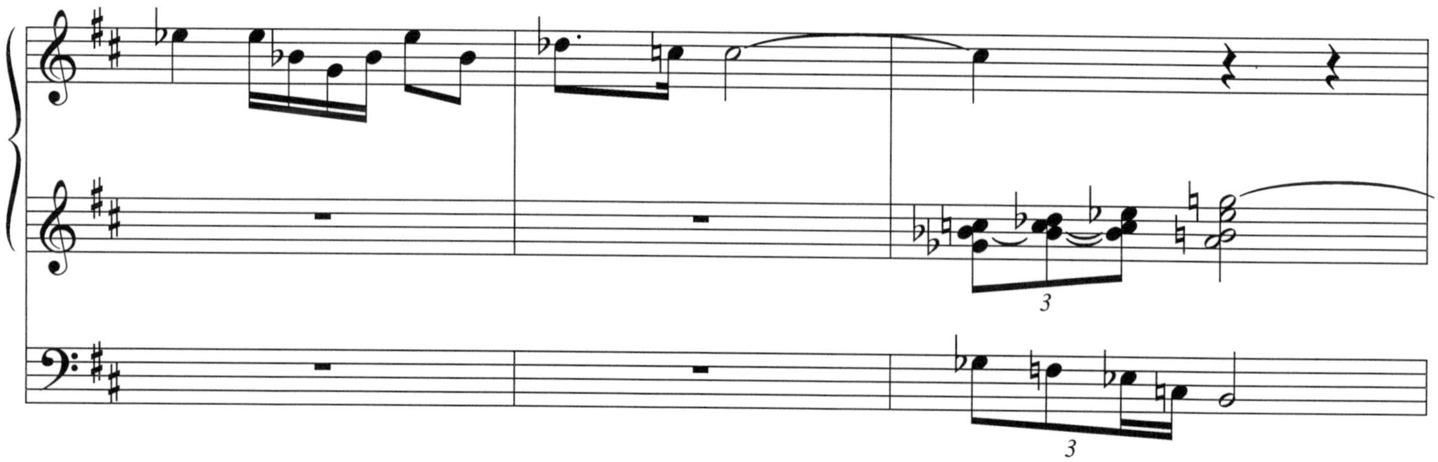

Freely
rit.
Solo Reed
mp
Reduce to Flutes
and Strings 8', 4'
p
Sw. Soft Strings
8va
pp
L.H.
Slowing
Solo
4' only

♩ = 76-80
Reed 16'
Flute 4', trem.
Flutes & Strings 8'

Light Principals 8', 4'
Registration as before

f
Add to Gt. & Sw.
Gt.
detached
rit.
a tempo
hold back
rit.

♩ = 80
ff
8va

Faster
loco
rit.
a tempo

tr
molto rit.
a tempo
Reed
fff
Gt.
Full Organ
rit.
fff

PEACE, PERFECT PEACE

GEORGE T. CALDBECK
Arranged by DIANE BISH

The highlight of my week was talking to Fred Bock on the telephone. He always had a joke or a funny story to tell, and our conversations were upbeat and sometimes hysterical. The use of credit cards in the piano (prepared piano a la John Cage), which, of course, "gave those unusual sounds," highly amused him. He would ask if I had any unused American Express Cards lying around, or perhaps even a Visa or a Mastercard. These, he said, would work too, but perhaps with not as good an audience "interest." Of course, Fred always wanted to make sure that "I was paying my proper tithe on any royalty checks I received."

Fred's musical output amazed me. It was so user and audience-friendly. It also had the touch of God's and Fred's spirit—oftentimes moving in nature, other times joyful and lighthearted. Throughout the good times and the bad times (earthquake), Fred's attitude toward life remained the same: peaceful and joyful. I am, therefore, happy to add "Peace, Perfect Peace" to this collection because it not only reflects the life of Christ, but it also reflects Christ's life in my friend and colleague, Fred Bock.

Sw. Oboe
Gt. Flutes 8', 4'
Ch. Strings
Ped. 16', 8', Ch. to Ped.

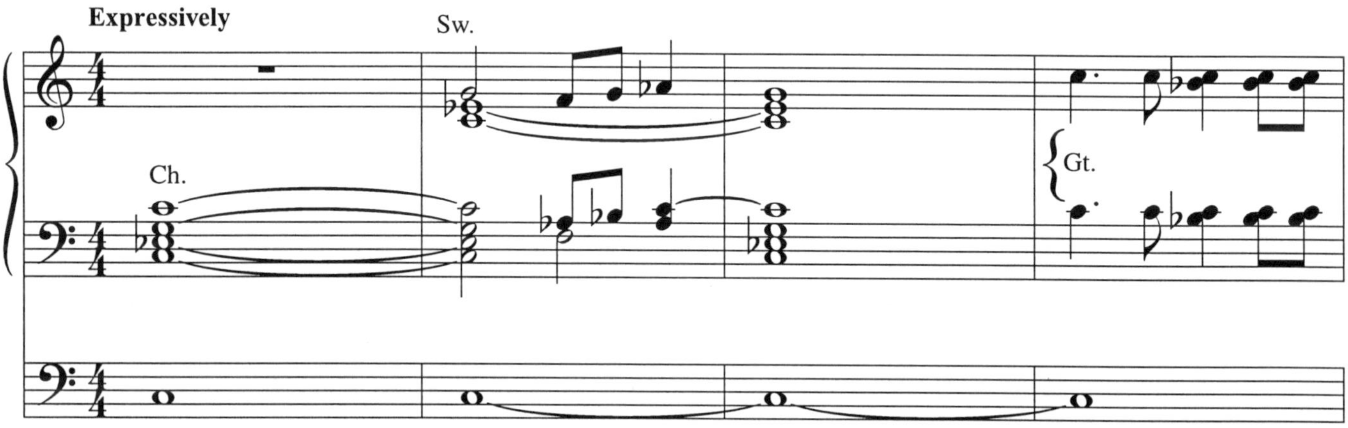

Gt.
Ch. Strings 16', 8', 4'
Ch.
+Bourdon 32'
Gt.
Gt. Flutes & Strings

Sw.
Sw. Strings

Sw. & Ch. Strings to Gt.
Gt.
Gt.
+ Sw. to Ped.
decresc.

Ch. Strings
Gt.
Ch.
Sw.
pppp

AT THE RIVER

ROBERT LOWRY
Arranged by GEORGE BAKER

Fred Bock cared deeply about two important things in life: friendship and family. When he became my publisher, I became his friend and part of his extended family. I will always remember his generous, loyal, and optimistic spirit. Fred loved a good laugh; I can still hear his deep and hearty roar in response to a funny story or joke. His musical tastes were impeccable; they were also practical and extremely usable. How we loved Fred Bock and how we miss him. Even so, we rejoice in this opportunity to honor him with a collection of new compositions.

Sw. Foundations 8'
Gt. Foundations 8'
Ch. Cornet 8'
Ped. Foundations 8'

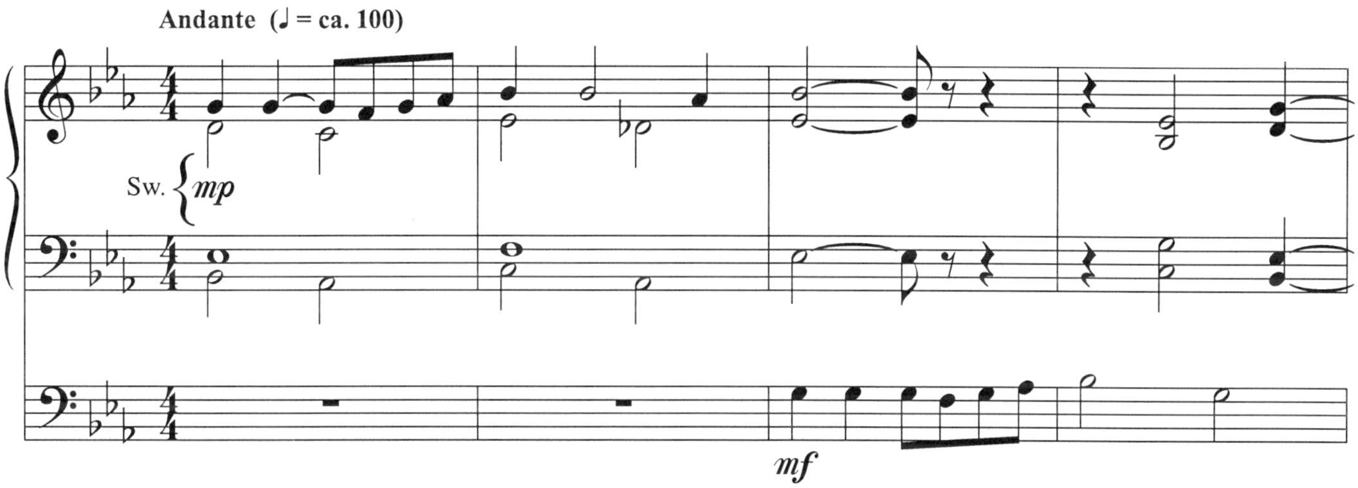

mf
Ch. to Ped. only
Ch.
mp
Sw. + Flute 4'
Sw.
mp
- Ch. to Ped.
+ Bourdon 8'
mf

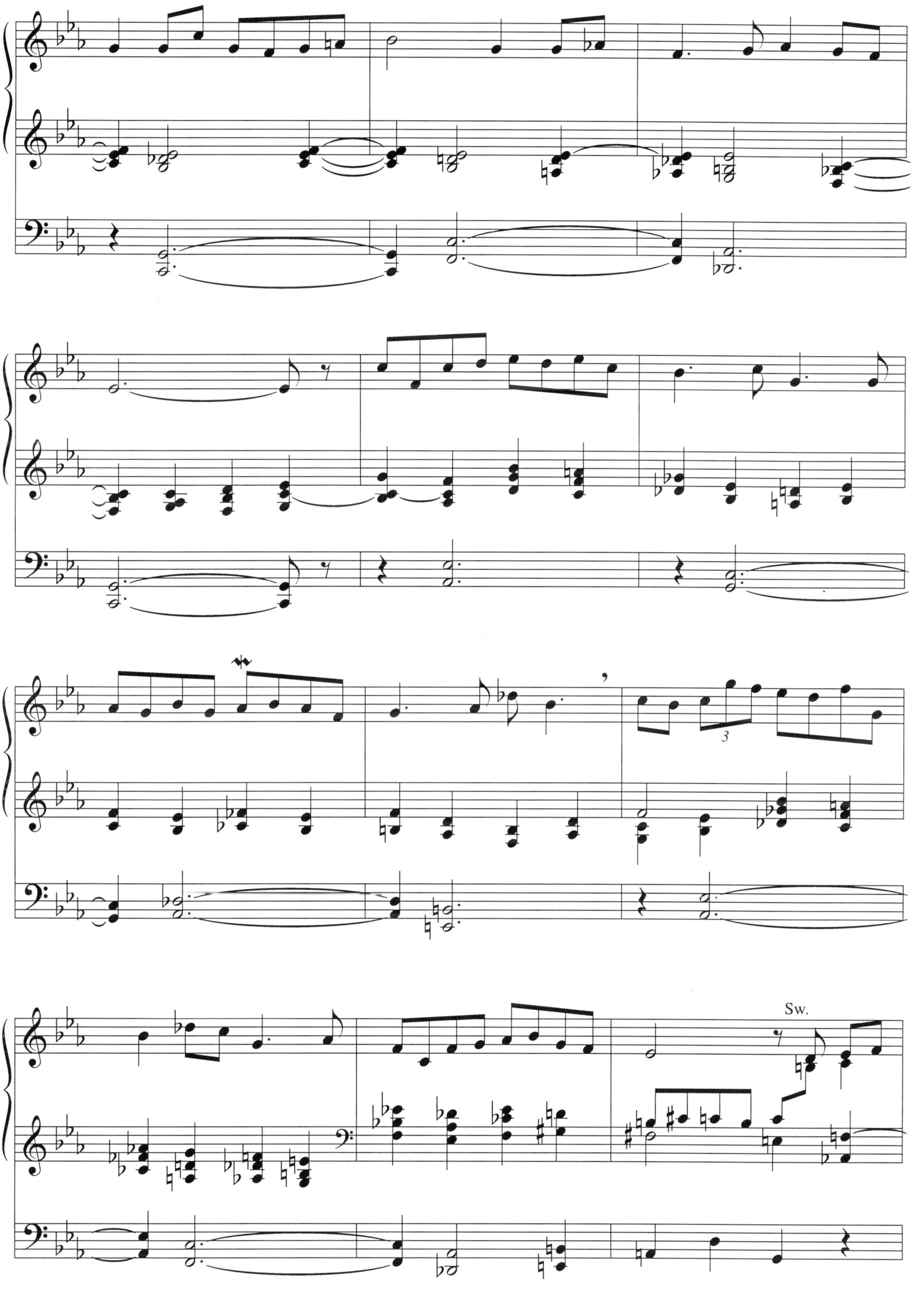
3
Sw.

cresc.
f
Gt., Sw., Ch.: Foundations 8'
+ All unison couplers
rit.
a tempo
Gt.
Foundations 16', 8'

Ch. 8', 2 2/3'
Tenderly
rit.
mp
Sw. Celeste 8'
p
Tempo I
Sw.
mp rit.
p molto rit.
pp
Bourdon 16'

LIFT HIGH THE CROSS

SYDNEY H. NICHOLSON
Arranged by CAROLYN HAMLIN

Fred Bock proved that one could live a happy, yet disciplined life. I learned early on that his delight in life's simple pleasures did not diminish his pursuit of excellence. In one conversation, Fred began by relating how much fun he had experienced that weekend water rafting with his son and ended by advising me to look again at the dynamics of my latest submission. His standards have proven invaluable as I sense his continuing critique of each manuscript. Fred wove the joy that permeated his life into his compositions. His legacy relates to that of Haydn's: "When I think upon God, my heart is so full of joy that the notes dance and leap, as it were, from my pen, and since God has given me a cheerful heart, it will be pardoned me that I serve Him with a cheerful spirit."

Carolyn Hamlin

Solo Enchamade 8'
Sw. Principals 8', 4', 2', Flutes 8', 4', 2', Sw. to Gt., Sw. to Ch., Sw. to Ped
Gt. Principals 8', 4', 2', Flutes 8', 4', 2', Mixtures, Gt. to Ped.
Ch. Principals 8', 4', 2', Flutes 8', 4', 2', Mixtures, Ch. to Gt.
Ped. Principals 16', 8', 4', Flutes 16', 8', 4'

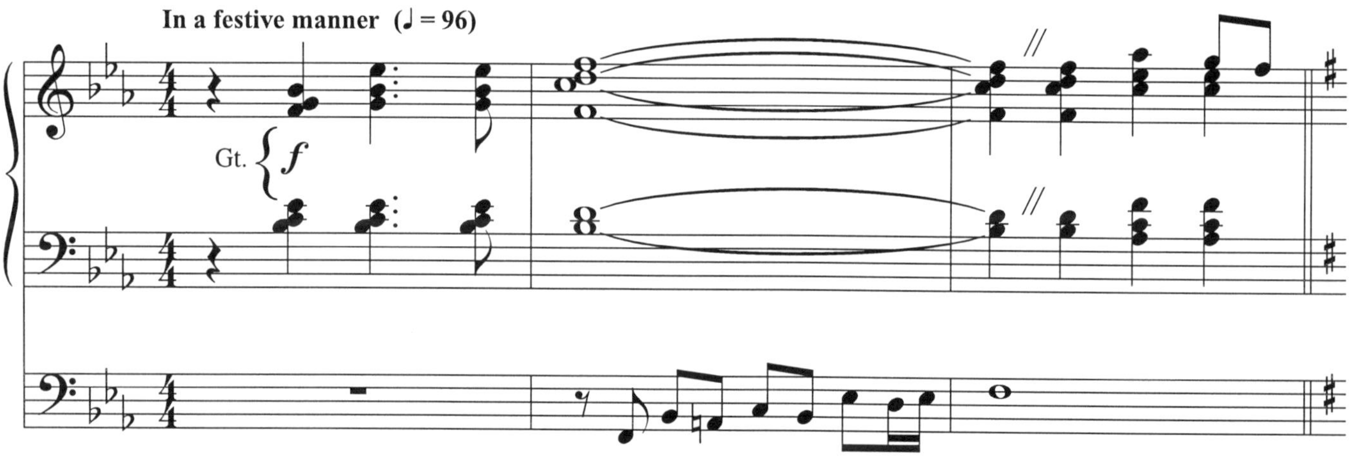

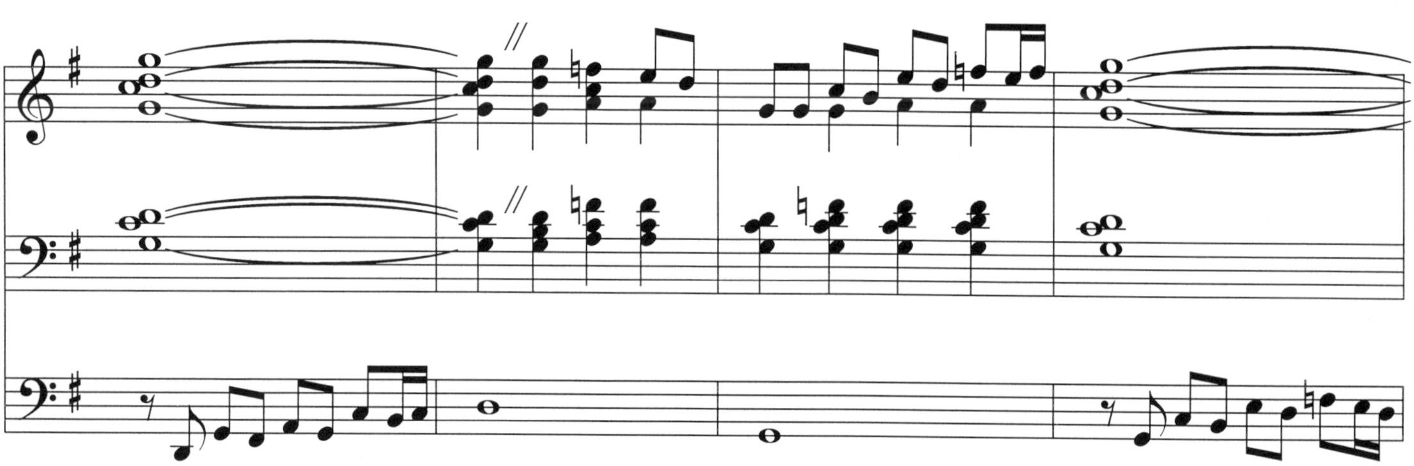

Solo
Ch.
mf

Solo
Gt.
Gt.

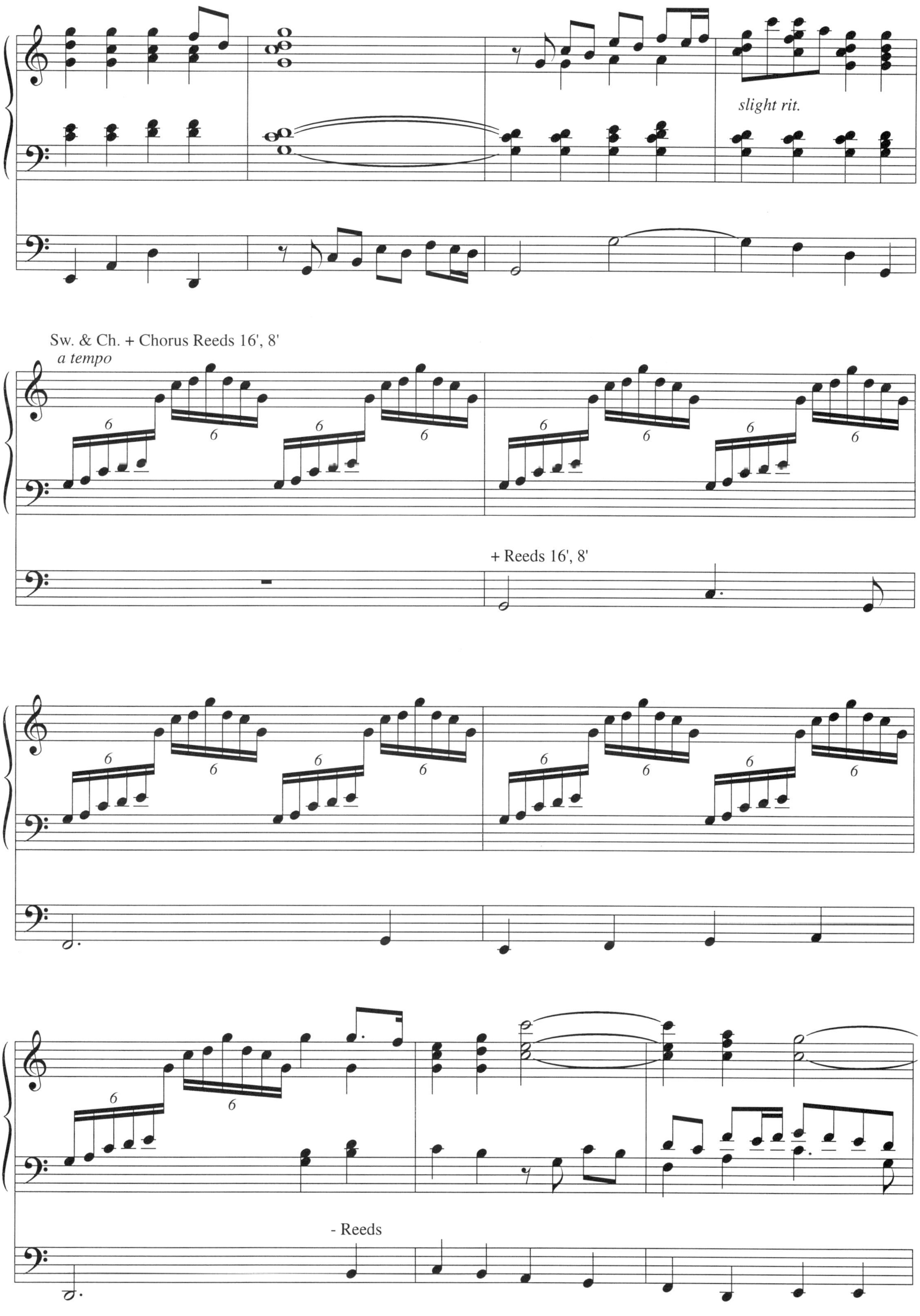
slight rit.
Sw. & Ch. + Chorus Reeds 16', 8'
a tempo
+ Reeds 16', 8'
- Reeds

+ Reeds
Gt. + Reeds 16', 8'
rit.

Full Organ with Reeds
+ 32' Reed
ff molto rit.

I WOULD BE TRUE

JOSEPH Y. PEEK
Arranged by CHRISTIAN ELLIOTT

So many thoughts come to mind when I think of Fred Bock and above all, the beauty of harmony in his compositions and arrangements. Fred was, after all, the master of "hot" chords! He also possessed a keen sense of humor which was reflected not only in his vibrant personality, but also made its way into his music. I marvel at the enormous productivity of this man who accomplished so much and whose work brought enormous joy and affected millions in a positive way.

Fred and I shared a keen interest in the theatre organ. Many of Fred's gospel arrangements reflected his love for well-tremulated pipes! While my setting of "I Would Be True" was not intended as a theatre organ style arrangement, Fred, I think, would say that the choice of chords and their voicings are "lush." It is offered as a sincere tribute to one whose creative genius inspired and lifted our spirits with beautiful music.

Comb. I Sw. Strings 8', Celestes
Gt. Harmonic Flute 8'
Ch. English Horn 8'
Ped. Light 16', 8' to balance manuals

Comb. II Sw. Diapason, Flute, Strings, Celestes 8', Flute 4', Vox Humana 8', Tremulant
Gt. Flutes, Diapasons 16', 8', 4', Tremulant, Sw. & Ch. to Gt. 16', 8', 4'
Ch. Strings, Celestes 8', Light Flutes 8', 4', Tremulant, Sw. to Ch. 8', 4'
Ped. Flutes 32', 16', 8', Ch. to Ped.

Gt.
Sw.
♩ = 92
French Horn
Clarinet

Comb. II
Gt.
cresc.
Ch.
cresc.

Comb. I
Gt.
Sw.
rit.
Ch. Strings
decresc. to end

Fred at Cadet Chapel, Westpoint Academy

A young Fred at an Easter Sunrise Service

Fred at City Temple, London

Fred at Bel Air Presbyterian Church

At a recording studio in Hollywood

Kimo Smith, Fred's Assistant, Ruth Case and Fred at Hollywood Presbyterian

Fred at the Mormon Tabernacle Organ

Fred at Dodger Stadium

Fred someplace in the world at some unknown organ

Fred at Crystal Cathedral

The Three B's,
Fred Bock, John Ness Beck and Hank Beebe
with Don Fontana

Fred at the Schlicker Organ, First Presbyterian Church, Hollywood

THE CROSS OF CHRIST

Arranged by JOYCE JONES

How does one write a short memory of a phenomenon like Fred Bock? A dedicated Christian, a fantastic arranger and composer, a successful publisher, a great inspiration to all who knew him—the descriptions could go on and on. Several years ago I asked Fred for program suggestions for a duo concert with pianist Kurt Kaiser, and Fred responded by sending us five books of his piano-organ arrangements! Each year we used one of Fred's medleys to begin our concert program. This past year we dedicated our performance to his memory. There will never be another like him.

Joyce Jones

Sw. Strings 8'
Gt. Flute 8'
Ch. Cromorne or Clarinet 8'
Ped. Gedeckt 16', 8'

*Music by George N. Allen

Sw.
Sw. - Strings, + Oboe
Gt. (or Ch. - Cromorne,
+ Gemshorn, Gems. Celeste)

*Music by Ithamar Conkey

(close swell box)
Sw. - Oboe, + Strings
Ch. Cromorne
(or Gt. + Flute 4')
Sw.

Sw.

in memory of my dear friend, Dr. Fred Bock

WHERE ALL IS PEACE

(Meditation on Two American Melodies)

Arranged by DR. KIMO SMITH

Fred was very proud of the honorary doctoral degree he received from Taylor University, so my customary greeting to him became, "Well, if it isn't Dr. Fred Bock" (appropriate emphasis on the "Dr."). Subsequently, when I received my doctorate from UCLA, he returned the favor by replying, "And if it isn't Dr. Kimo Smith!" The credits here reflect both the humor we enjoyed and the sincere mutual admiration that we shared.

Sw. Flutes 8', 4', 2 2/3'
Ch. Flutes and Strings
Ped. Solo Reed 4'

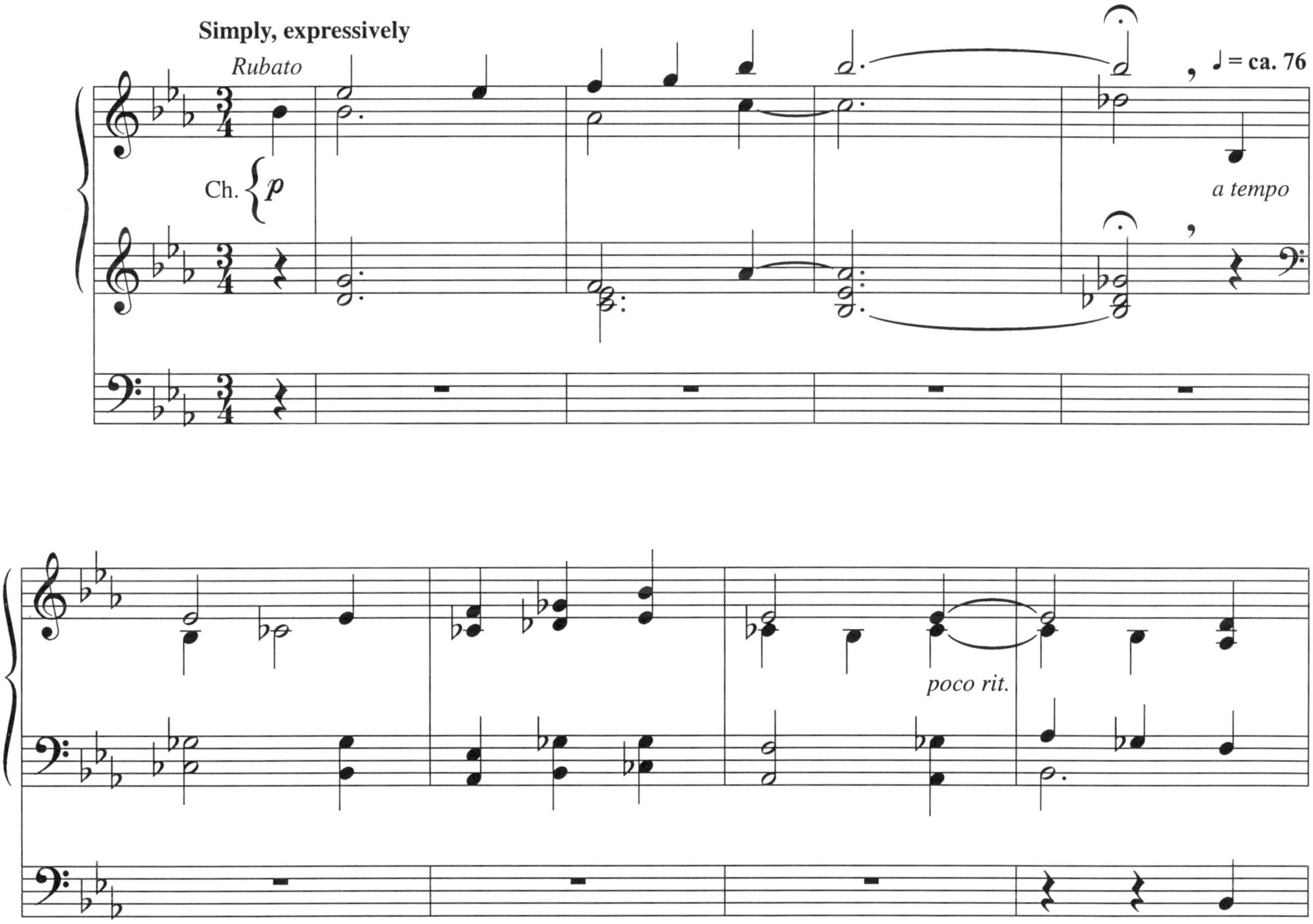

"Jerusalem, My Happy Home" (Trad.)
a tempo

- Reed
+ 16', 8'
"Deep River" (Trad.)
Sw.
Add to Ch.

Ch.
mf
piu mosso
poco rit.
Slower
Ch. Flutes, Strings
p
poco cresc.
dim.
rit.
Sw.
a tempo
Ch. legato
- 16', 8'
+Solo Reed or Principal 8'

poco rit.
Ch.
p
- Solo
+ 16', 8'
Ch. Strings only
pp

FANTASY ON HYFRYDOL

ROWLAND H. PRICHARD
Arranged by MARK THALLANDER

I first met Fred Bock in the late 1970's at a festival service in the former sanctuary of Garden Grove Community Church (now The Crystal Cathedral). Don Fontana, the Minister of Music, had creatively designed a program that featured the music of the three "B's": John Ness Beck, Hank Beebe, and Fred Bock. It was an electric event with all three composers in attendance!

Then in the summer of 1982, Fred was the guest organist one Sunday for the morning worship services at The Crystal Cathedral. Fred played the newly installed Ruffatti Pipe Organ magnificently. After I heard his "Praise God," both as an organ arrangement and as a choral setting, it became one of my favorites.

In the years that followed, Fred and I continued to have many opportunities for ministry and fellowship. The multi-faceted dimensions of his life and work enriched me both professionally and personally. I am humbled and honored to have known him and look forward to the day when I will once again experience Fred's special gift of joy!

Mark Thallander

Sw., Gt., Ch., Pos. Full to Mixtures
Ped. Full to Reeds

Triumphantly (♩ = 126)

Loco
Add Manual Reeds
(boxes closed)
mf
cresc.
f

rit. Add
ff a tempo

8va

Loco
Full
rit.
En Chamade

SPIRIT OF GOD, DESCEND UPON MY HEART

FREDERICK C. ATKINSON
Arranged by JAN SANBORN

Fred Bock was an amazing businessman who possessed a deep faith with which he wholeheartedly served God. He was also one of the funniest men I have ever known. From the day that he introduced himself to me after a Youth for Christ rally, he enriched my life as well as the lives of those around me.

It is an honor for me to be remembered as the one who introduced him to my friend, Lois, his wife of 34 years. Today, she and I work together on the Editorial Board of the Fred Bock Music Company. Who could have imagined? But then who could have imagined that a tragedy would prematurely take a man of such great creativity and imagination from us?

I hope that my continued service to the Lord will also be a tribute to Fred's life. My contribution to this book includes some harmonic progressions that he might have enjoyed. I hope that you, the performer, will enjoy them as well and that they will inspire you as you play.

Sw. French Horn, or similar solo stop
Gt. Principal 16', 8'
Ch. Strings, Celeste
Ped. Flute 16', 8', Ch. to Ped.

Gt.
Sw.
Ch.
mp
Gt. Princ. 8', 4'
Add
mf

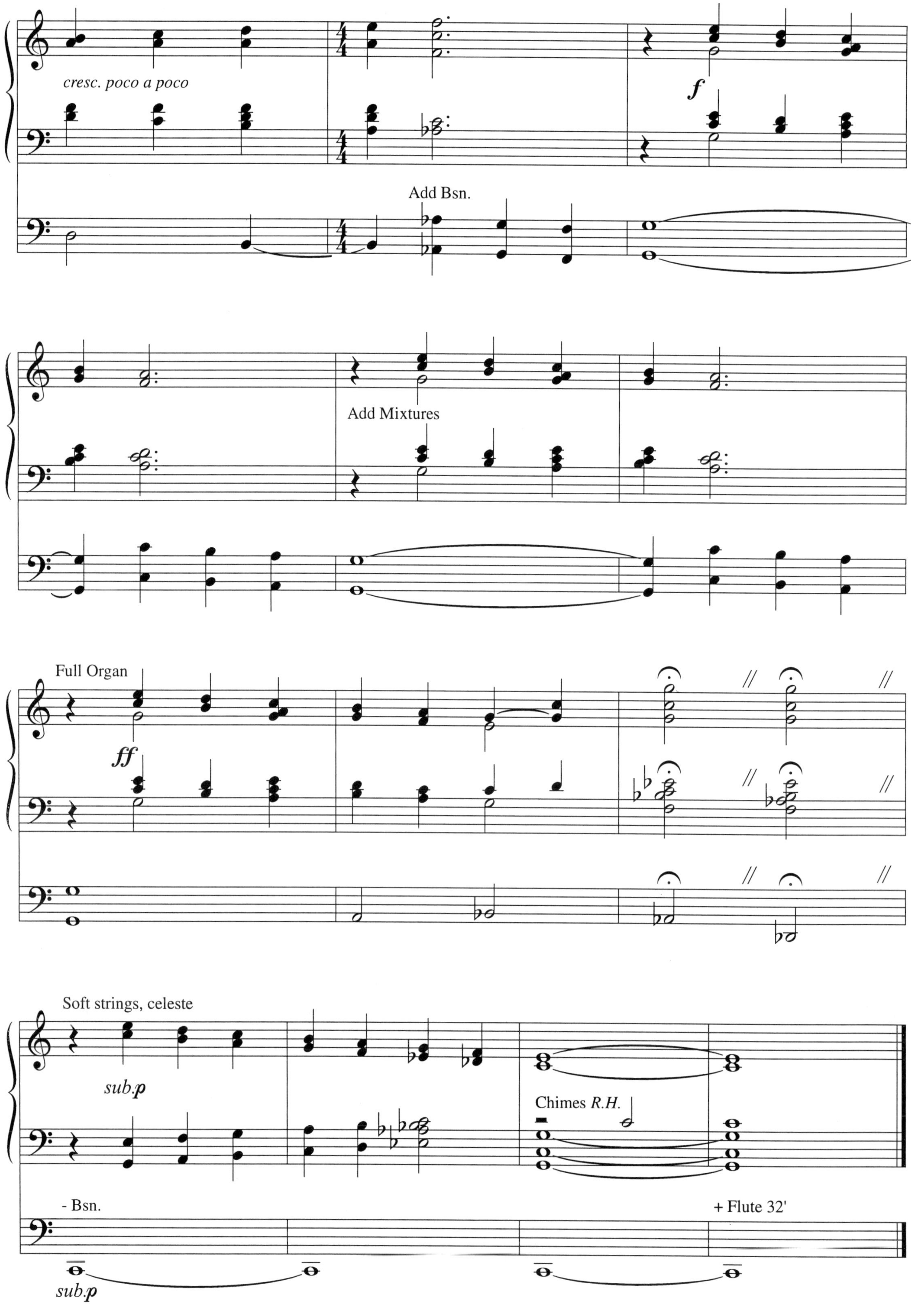
cresc. poco a poco
f
Add Bsn.
Add Mixtures
Full Organ
ff
Soft strings, celeste
sub.p
Chimes R.H.
- Bsn.
+ Flute 32'
sub.p

NICAEA
(Holy, Holy, Holy)

Based on the tune by
John Baccus Dykes (1823-1876)
CRAIG PHILLIPS

In 1995, Fred Bock called me "out of the blue" because a collection of hymn-tune preludes that I wrote in the 1980s had gone out of print. He wondered if I would be interested in allowing his company to re-release it. He was especially taken with the setting of "Lobe den Herren," which he had heard Kimo Smith play at Hollywood Presbyterian Church. Subsequently, Fred sent me programs from the church whenever my music was performed. I was touched and flattered because as a young student, I had known and admired Fred's hymn-tune settings of the 1970's. Delighted, I agreed to the re-release. In 1997, Fred took me to lunch and presented me with the new "baby," as he referred to the collection.

Unexpectedly, our paths crossed again on August 16, 1997, when I played for a wedding at St. Brenden's Church in Los Angeles. Back-to-back weddings were scheduled, and just as I finished the recessional music, the next wedding party took over. As I turned to leave, there stood Fred. "What are you doing here?" I asked. His son was getting married! What a proud and happy man he was on that August day. Neither of us knew that it would be our final earthly meeting.

Sw. Full with Reeds
Gt. Principal Chorus, Sw. and Ch. to Gt.
Ch. Foundations, Sw. to Ch.
Ped. Full with Reeds, Manuals to Ped.

Allegro moderato e marcato (♩ = ca. 76)

Brilliante
L.H.
legato
detaché

Ch.
Sw.
mf
Gt.
Ch.
- Reeds
tr
Gt. (or big Solo Reed 8')
Sw.

poco rit.
Ch.
L.H.
f
Gt.
a tempo
+ Reeds

sempre marcato
allarg.
ff a tempo
+ Reed 32'
5

allarg.
tr
3
3

Do You Have These Other Fred Bock Organ Books?

The Organ Music of Fred Bock #1

BG0889

Contents

Prelude on *BE THOU MY VISION*
Prelude on *JESUS, THOU JOY OF LOVING HEARTS*
Prelude on *THE LORD'S MY SHEPHERD*
Prelude on *MORNING HAS BROKEN*
Postlude on *NOW THANK WE ALL OUR GOD*
Fantasia on *ON CHRISTMAS NIGHT*

The Organ Music of Fred Bock #2

BG0914

Contents

ANGELS, FROM THE REALMS OF GLORY
ANGELS WE HAVE HEARD ON HIGH
I WONDER AS I WANDER
INFANT HOLY, INFANT LOWLY
JOY TO THE WORLD
O COME, ALL YE FAITHFUL
O LITTLE TOWN OF BETHLEHEM
SILENT NIGHT
THE FIRST NOEL
THOU DIDST LEAVE THY THRONE